The universe is full of surprises: strange planets, black holes, objects traveling at fast speeds, faraway stars...

Do you want to learn some of its most amazing facts?

LET'S GET STARTED!

THE MILKY WAY

The universe contains billions of galaxies.

One of them is the Milky Way. It is the one where we live.

It owes its name to the fact that its extension through the sky has the appearance of a milky path.

Its origin comes from Greek mythology. Hermes took Heracles, son of Zeus, to be breastfed by Hera while she slept. Upon awakening, she pushed Heracles away, pouring out the milk above the firmament.

MILLION OF STARS

Do you know how many stars are there in the Milky Way?

Scientists believe that there might be at least a hundred billion stars in our galaxy. Yes, 100,000,000,000!

Each one of those stars is like a Sun. Although with different sizes.

THE OTHER PLANETS

Thanks to new technological advances, it is being shown that almost all stars have planets orbiting around them, just like in our solar system.

If there are thousands of millions of stars... imagine how many planets there are in the universe!

Earth and the other planets orbit around the Sun.

EARTH SPEED

Surely you already know that Earth takes one year, 365 days, to make a circle around the Sun.

But do you know the speed that our planet travels while making that journey?

Earth makes an elliptical orbit around the Sun at an average speed of 67,000 mph (107,000 km/h).

THE SUNLIGHT

Do you know that there is nothing in the universe that travels faster than the speed of light?

It does so at 186,000 miles/sec (300,000 km/s).

Knowing that the average distance between the Sun and the Earth is 93 million miles (150,000,000 km), we know that its light takes about 8 minutes to reach our planet.

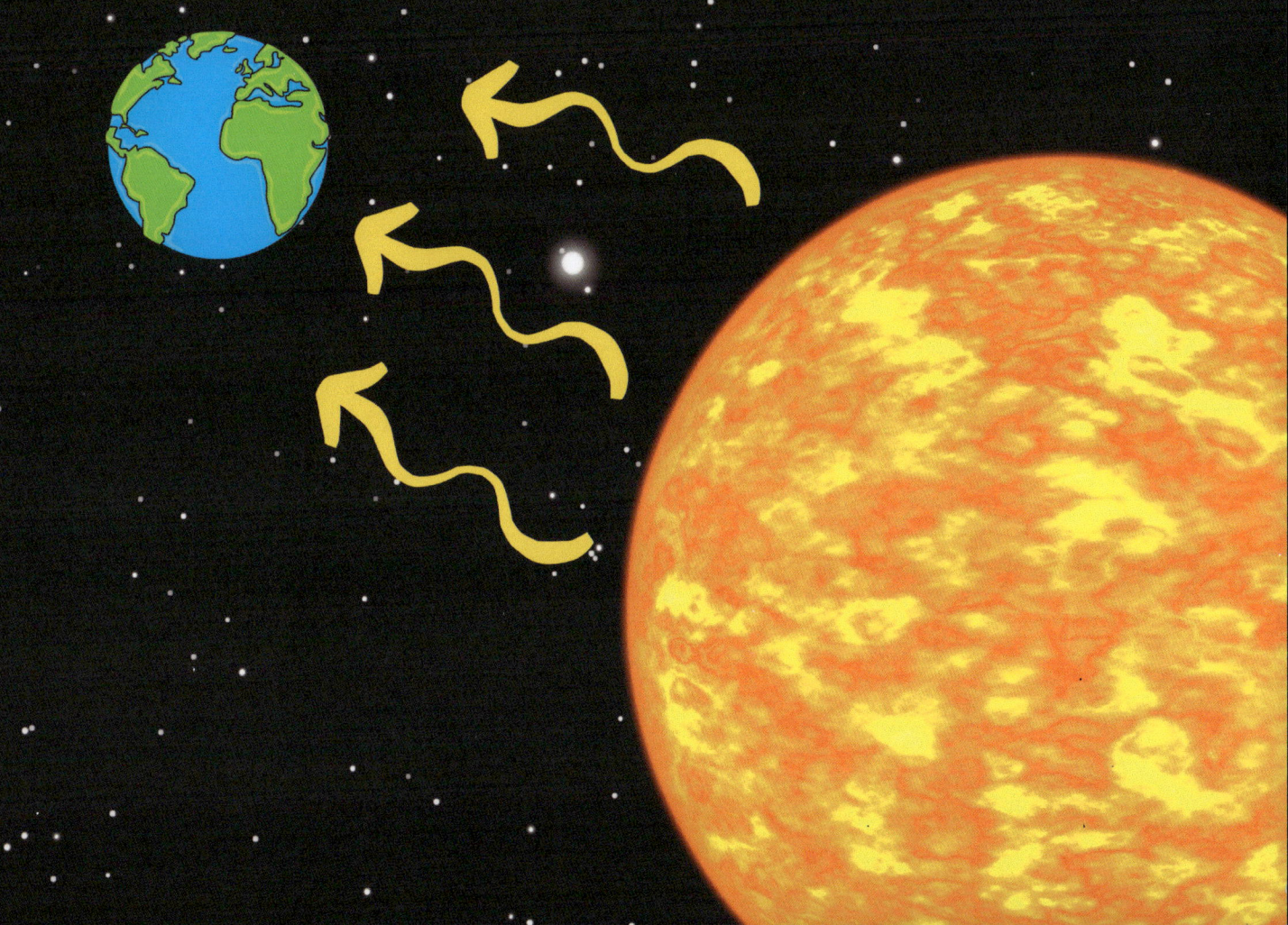

If the Sun went out, it would take us 8 minutes to notice!

A GLANCE AT THE PAST

Therefore, looking at the stars is like traveling back in time, looking at the past.

Considering the distance of some of them (million light-years away), we might be seeing something that could have actually disappeared a long time ago.

THE CENTER OF OUR GALAXY

Could you tell me what is in the center of our galaxy?

There is a supermassive black hole at the center of the Milky Way. It's called Sagittarius A*.

It is believed that most, if not all, galaxies are home to a supermassive black hole at their center.

Black holes are areas in space with a huge gravitational field. Everything that approaches is absorbed and nothing can escape from them, not even light!

PLANETS OF THE SOLAR SYSTEM

Our solar system consists of 8 planets:

You probably knew that already. But did you know that aside from those planets, there are **5 dwarf planets** in our solar system?

Pluto

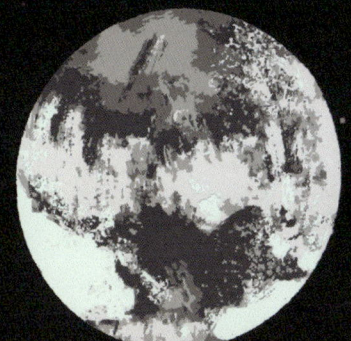
Eris

Haumea

Makemake

Ceres

THE DIFFERENT TYPES OF PLANETS

We can differentiate two types among the planets in our solar system:

- Rocky
- Gas giant

Rocky: they are distinguished by having a mostly solid surface. They are Mercury, Venus, Earth, and Mars.

Gas giants: they are formed mainly of gas and a small solid nucleus. These are the furthest from the Sun: Jupiter, Saturn, Uranus, and Neptune

THE NAKED EYE PLANETS

From Earth, before sunrise, we can see 5 of the planets in our solar system with the naked eye. The planets visible to the naked eye are Mercury, Venus, Mars, Jupiter, and Saturn.

The naked eye means that they can be seen without the assistance of optical instruments, using just the eyes.

IS IT A STAR OR A PLANET?

Could you differentiate a star from a planet in the sky?

The first thing you should know is that the **stars are the only ones that twinkle**, while the planets are seen as a fixed light in the sky.

Thus, you just have to analyze their brightness. All the stars twinkle at night, but not so with the planets. Their light reaches us continuously, without twinkling.

A VERY HOT PLANET

Could you tell me which is the hottest planet in the solar system?

You are probably thinking of Mercury since it is the closest to the Sun. But the truth is that the hottest planet is Venus.

This is due to its dense atmosphere full of carbon dioxide, which leads to a strong greenhouse effect, and its clouds formed by sulfuric acid

The temperature on Venus reaches 860 °F (460 °C) on average. How hot!

BYE, MOON!

As you might already know, Earth has a satellite that orbits around it: the Moon.

The average distance between Earth and the Moon is 238,855 miles (384,400 km).

Did you know that the Moon moves away from Earth almost 1.5 inches (3.82 cm)?

That means that, a long time ago, the Moon was closer to Earth, and in the future, we will see it farther away from us.

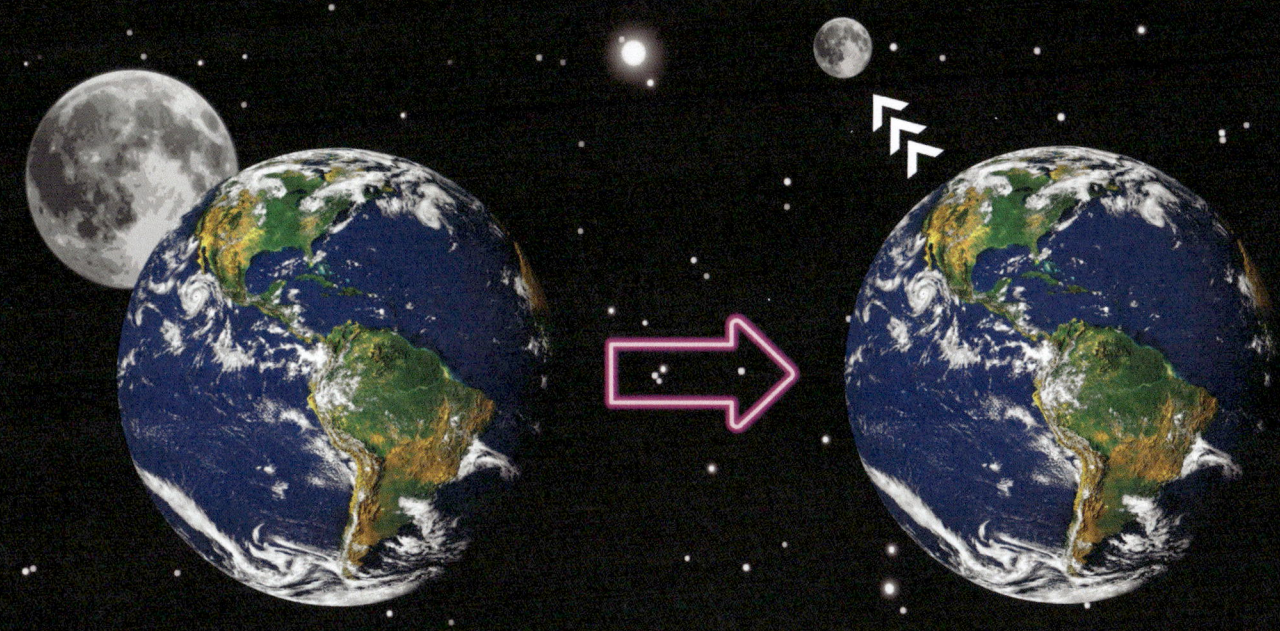

THE OTHER MOONS

Just like we, the inhabitants of the planet Earth, have a satellite that orbits around us, other planets have their own satellites as well.

Saturn is the planet within our solar system with the most satellites or moons.

It has 83 moons with confirmed orbits, although it could be said that it has about 200 if we count those that are immersed in its rings.

WATER OUTSIDE EARTH

Until recently it seemed impossible to imagine the existence of water outside Earth. Recent studies are making it possible to find water outside our planet, in places such as the Moon, Mars, and some satellites of Jupiter and Saturn.

These findings are very important because the existence of water gives hope as regards the idea of a discovery of life outside Earth.

Beware! The fact that life is discovered in those places does not mean that there are extraterrestrial beings! It could be, for instance, microscopic life. Or remains of already extinct life could also be discovered.

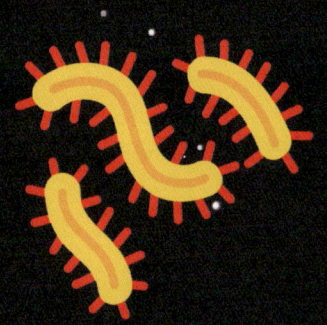 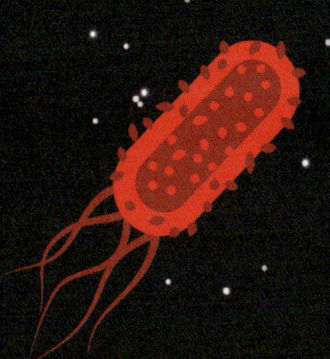 

PLANETS LIKE EARTH?

Astronomers have estimated that there could be 6 million Earth-like planets just in the Milky Way.

These planets are rocky, have the same size as Earth, and orbit in the habitable zone of a star.

Habitable zone: The distance of a planet from its star (its sun) would allow the existence of liquid water and hence the possibility of life.

The water would evaporate from the heat if it were closer to its star. And in the case of being too far away, the water would be in a solid state (ice).

COMETS VS ASTEROIDS?

Could you differentiate a comet from an asteroid?

The truth is that they are very similar. **The main difference is the material they are made of.**

Asteroids are made of rock and metal. Comets are made of rock, ice, and organic material.

Comets are distinguished by their tail, which asteroids lack. This is due to their composition. As they approach the Sun, comets heat up and give off gas and dust, giving shape to their tails.

Asteroid   Comet

A HUGE DIAMOND IN SPACE

Years ago, astronomers discovered a diamond the size of the Moon in space.

It is actually a **white dwarf**, a star that has run out of fuel. The star turned into crystallized carbon (diamond) through the cooling process.

This huge diamond is known as Lucy, after the famous Beatles song, Lucy in the sky with diamonds. However, its real name is BPM 37093.

A VERY QUIET PLACE

Did you know that there is no sound in space?

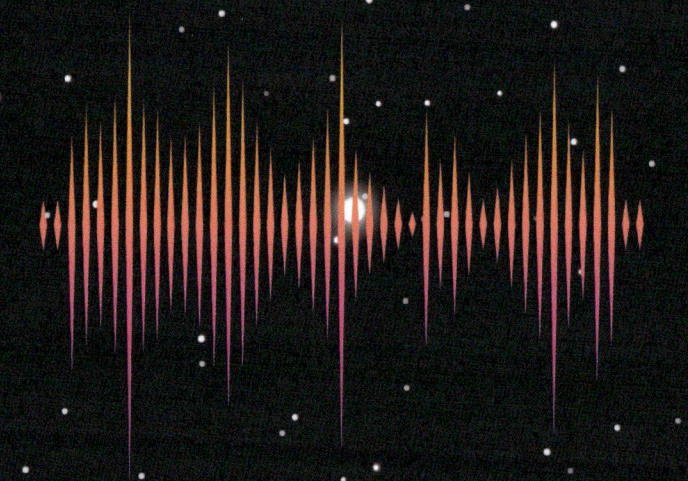

This is because sound needs a medium to travel through. Usually, it does so through the air.

The space is a vacuum with no air, and for this reason, the sound is not transmitted.

So, no one could hear your screams in space! 😱

And we come to the end.

The universe is certainly a place full of mysteries and amazing things.

New discoveries are made every day. It will be very interesting to know what new data we obtain, from now on, from this immense place of which we are a small part.

I hope you liked it and that you learned new things.

I want to ask you a favor so that this book reaches more people, and that is that you rate it with a sincere opinion on the platform where you purchased it.

With that small gesture, you will be helping me to carry on with new projects.

I can't wait to start creating my next book for you!

See you soon!

Books

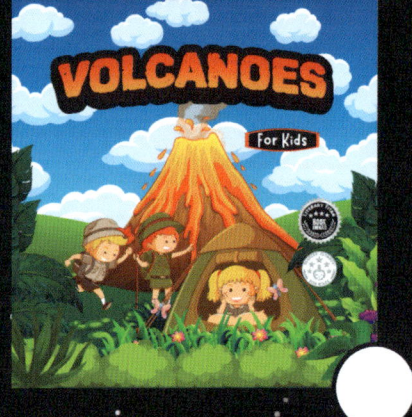

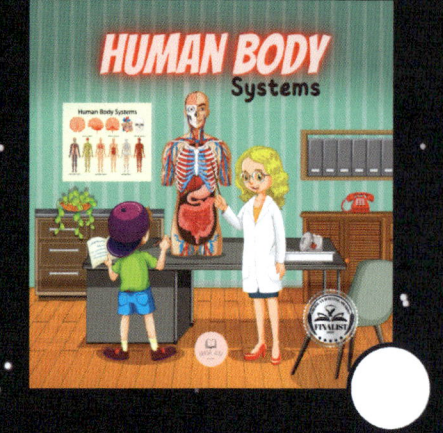

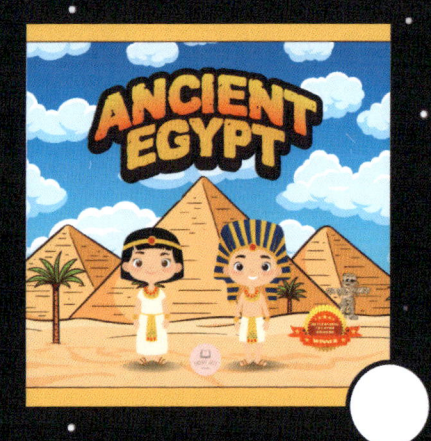

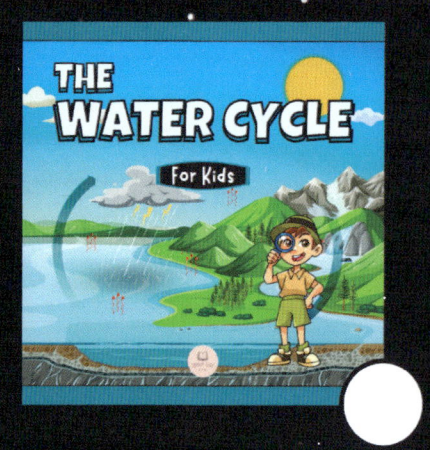

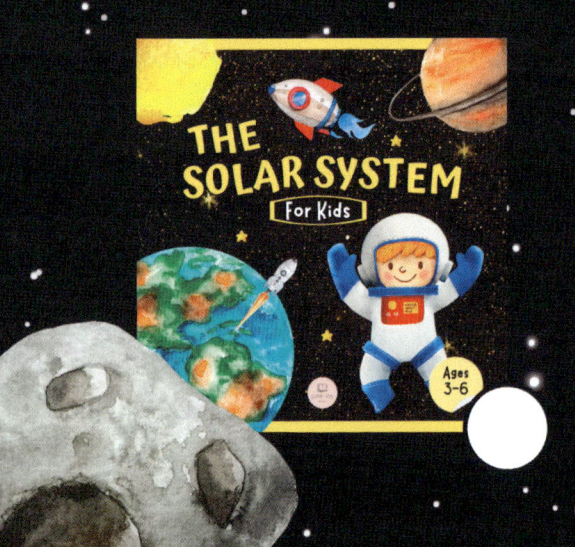

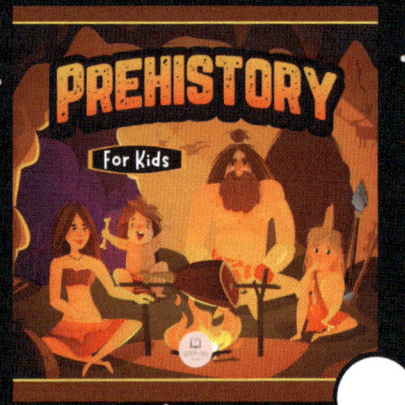

- ✓ Fascinating Universe Facts
- ○ Volcanoes For Kids
- ○ Human Body Systems
- ○ The Most Famous Landmarks in the World
- ○ Ancient Egypt
- ○ The Water Cycle For Kids
- ○ The Solar System For Kids (Ages 3-6)
- ○ Prehistory For Kids

SCAN ME

Printed in Great Britain
by Amazon